FORT SUMTER

*National Monument
South Carolina*

by Frank Barnes

NATIONAL PARK SERVICE HISTORICAL HANDBOOK SERIES NO. 12
WASHINGTON, D. C., 1952

(Revised 1962)

The National Park System, of which Fort Sumter National Monument is a unit, is dedicated to conserving the scenic, scientific, and historic heritage of the United States for the benefit and enjoyment of its people.

Contents

	Page
CONSTRUCTION OF FORT SUMTER	1
MAJOR ANDERSON MOVES GARRISON FROM MOULTRIE TO SUMTER	6
THE STAR OF THE WEST	8
PREPARATIONS FOR WAR	9
LINCOLN ORDERS A RELIEF EXPEDITION TO FORT SUMTER	10
THE CONFEDERATES DEMAND FORT SUMTER'S EVACUATION	13
THE WAR BEGINS—APRIL 12, 1861	15
CHARLESTON AND THE FEDERAL BLOCKADE—1861-63	24
FEDERAL IRONCLADS ATTACK FORT SUMTER	24
THE MORRIS ISLAND APPROACH TO FORT SUMTER	26
THE FIRST GREAT BOMBARDMENT OF FORT SUMTER	28
THE SMALL-BOAT ASSAULT	32
THE SECOND GREAT BOMBARDMENT	33
STALEMATE—SPRING OF 1864	35
FORT SUMTER STRENGTHENED	36
THE THIRD GREAT BOMBARDMENT	36
SHERMAN'S MARCH FORCES SUMTER'S EVACUATION	38
MAJOR ANDERSON RETURNS	38
FORT SUMTER AFTER 1865	40
GUIDE TO THE AREA	42
ADMINISTRATION	46
RELATED AREAS	46
SUGGESTED READINGS	47

The housetops in Charleston during the bombardment of April 12–13, 1861. From Harper's Weekly, May 4, 1861.

AT 4:30 A. M., APRIL 12, 1861, a mortar battery at Fort Johnson fired a shell that burst directly over Fort Sumter. This was the signal for a general bombardment by the Confederate batteries about Charleston Harbor. For 34 hours, April 12 and 13, Fort Sumter was battered with shot and shell. Then the Federal commander, Maj. Robert Anderson, agreed to evacuate; and, on April 14, he and his small garrison departed with the full honors of war. On the following day, President Abraham Lincoln issued a call for 75,000 militia. The tragedy of the American Civil War had begun.

Two years later, Fort Sumter, now a Confederate stronghold, became the scene of a stubborn defense. From April 1863 to February 1865 its garrison withstood a series of devastating bombardments and direct attacks by Federal forces from land and sea. Fort Sumter was evacuated only when Federal forces bypassed Charleston from the rear. At the end, buttressed with sand and cotton as well as its own fallen brick and masonry, it was stronger than ever militarily. And it had become a symbol of resistance and courage for the entire South.

Both the "first shot" of April 1861 and the long siege of 1863–65 are commemorated today by Fort Sumter National Monument.

Construction of Fort Sumter

". . . the character of the times particularly inculcates the lesson that, whether to prevent or repel danger, we ought not to be unprepared for it. This consideration will sufficiently recommend to Congress a liberal provision for the immediate extension and gradual completion of the works of defense, both fixed and floating, on our maritime frontier. . . ."

—President Madison to Congress,
December 5, 1815.

The War of 1812 had shown the gross inadequacy of the coastal defenses of the United States. The crowning indignity had been the burning of Washington. Accordingly, Congress now answered President Madison's call by setting up a military Board of Engineers for Seacoast Fortifications to devise a new system of national defense. Brig. Gen. Simon Bernard, the famed military engineer of Napoleon, was commissioned in the Corps of Engineers and assigned to the Board. Under his unofficial direction, the Board began surveying the entire coast line of the United States in 1817. The South Atlantic coast, "especially regarded as less important," was not surveyed until 1821. One fortification report, covering the Gulf coast and the Atlantic coast between Cape Hatteras and the St. Croix River, had been submitted to Congress earlier that year. Thus, not till the revised form of this report was submitted to Congress in 1826 was the possibility that the "shoal opposite [Fort Moultrie] may be occupied permanently" officially broached. This was the genesis of Fort Sumter. If the location were feasible, reported the Board, "the fortification of the harbor may be considered as an easy and simple problem." With the guns of the projected fort crossing fire with those of Fort

The rock-ring of Fort Sumter's foundation as it looked 4 years after operations were begun. Courtesy National Archives.

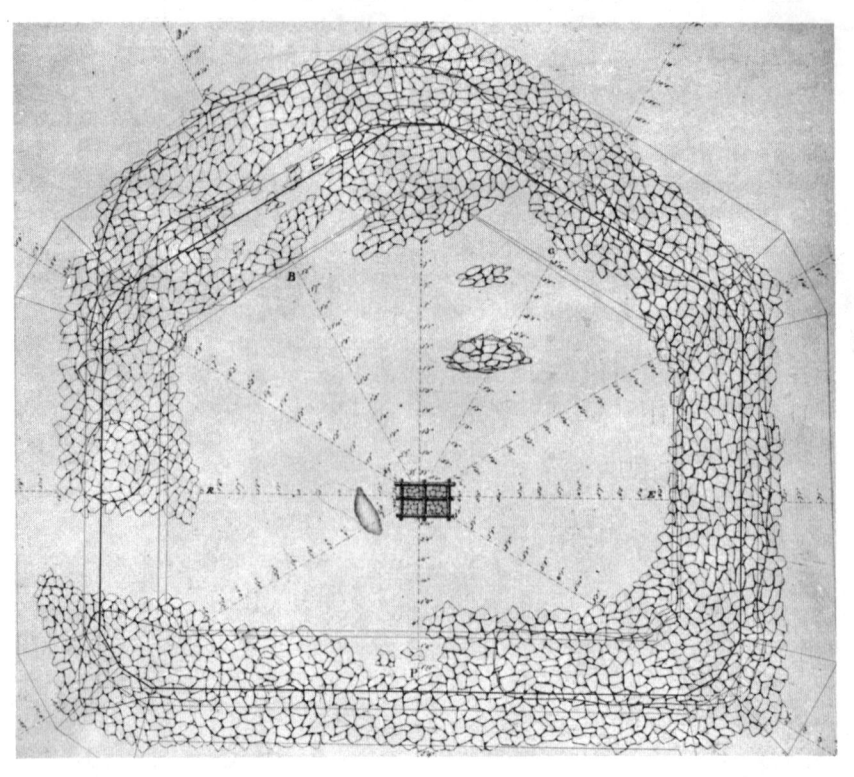

Moultrie, the commercial city of Charleston would be most effectively protected against attack.

Plans for the new fort were drawn up in 1827 and adopted on December 5, 1828. In the course of that winter Lt. Henry Brewerton, Corps of Engineers, assumed charge of the project and active operations were commenced. Progress was slow, however, and as late as 1834 the new fort was no more than a hollow pentagonal rock "mole" 2 feet above low water and open at one side to permit supply ships to pass to the interior. Meanwhile, it had been named Sumter in honor of Thomas Sumter, of South Carolina, the "Gamecock" of the Revolution.

Late in the autumn of 1834 operations were suddenly suspended. Ownership of the site was in question. In the preceding May, one William Laval, resident of Charleston, had secured from the State a conveniently vague grant to 870 acres of "land" in Charleston Harbor. In November, acting under this grant, Laval notified the representative of the United States Engineers at Fort Johnson of his claim to the site of Fort Sumter. In the meantime, the South Carolina Legislature had become curious about the operations in Charleston Harbor. Late in

First-floor plan, Fort Sumter, March 1861. The Gorge (designed for officers' quarters) is at the base of the plan. Gun casemates line the other four sides. The fort magazines were at either extremity of the Gorge in both casemate tiers. Courtesy National Archives.

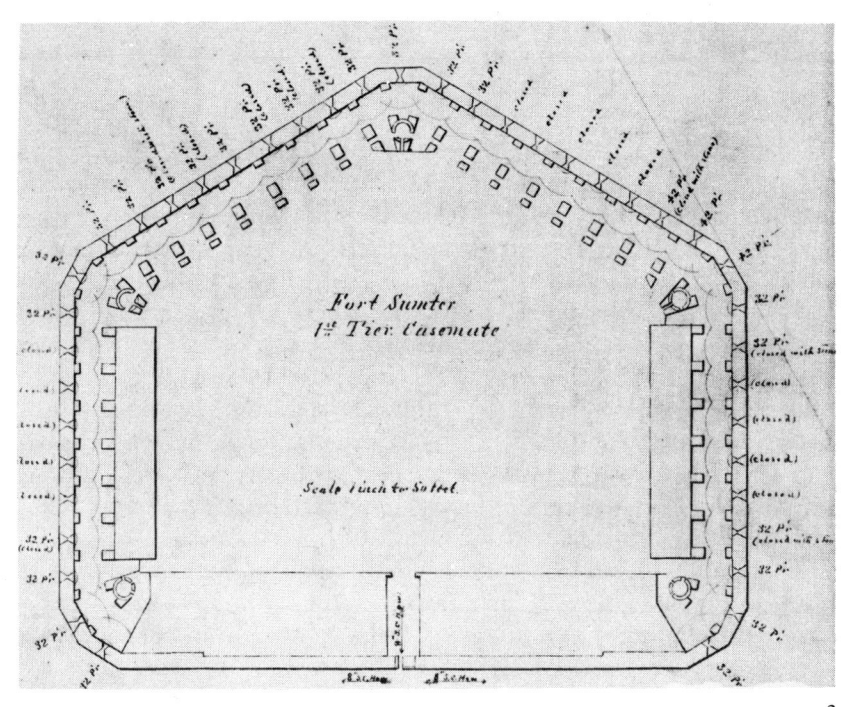

November, inquiry had been instituted as to "whether the creation of an Island on a shoal in the Channel, may not injuriously affect the navigation and commerce of [Charleston] Harbor. . . ." Reporting the following month, the Committee on Federal Relations had made the ominous pronouncement that they had not "been able to ascertain by what authority the Government have assumed to erect the works alluded to. . . ." Apparently under the impression that a formal deed of cession to "land" ordinarily covered with water had not been necessary, the Federal Government had commenced operations at the mouth of Charleston Harbor without consulting the State of South Carolina.

It was not until January 1841 that work was resumed on the site of Fort Sumter. Laval's claim was invalidated by the State attorney general under act of the South Carolina Legislature, December 20, 1837. But the harbor issue remained and was complicated still further by a memorial presented to the legislature by James C. Holmes, Charleston lawyer, on that same date. Not before November 22, 1841, was the Federal Government's title to 125 acres of harbor "land" recorded in the office of the Secretary of State of South Carolina.

Under the skilful guidance of Capt. A. H. Bowman, the work was now pushed forward. The original plans were changed in several respects. Perhaps the most important modification was with respect to the foundation. Instead of a "grillage of continuous square timbers" upon the rock mass, Bowman's idea of laying several courses of granite blocks was adopted, in the main. Bowman had feared the complete destruction of the wood by worms; and palmetto, which might have resisted such attack, had not the compactness of fiber or the necessary strength to support the weight of the superstructure.

The work was difficult. The granite of the foundation, for example, was laid between high and low watermarks, and there were periods of time when the tide permitted no work to be done at all. Yellow fever was a recurrent problem; so was the excessive heat of the Charleston summers. Much of the building material had to be brought in from the north. The magnitude of the task is indicated by the quantities involved: about 10,000 tons of granite (some of it from as far away as the Penobscot River region in Maine) and well over 60,000 tons of other rock. Bricks, shells, and sand could be obtained locally, but even here there were problems. Local brickyard capacities were small and millions of bricks were required. Similarly, hundreds of thousands of bushels of shells were needed—for concrete, for the foundation of the first-tier casemate floors, and for use in the parade fill next to the enrockment. Even the actual delivery of supplies, however local in origin, was a problem, for then, as now, Fort Sumter was a difficult spot at which to land.

Fort Sumter in December 1860 was a five-sided brick masonry fort designed for three tiers of guns. Its 5-foot-thick outer walls, towering nearly 50 feet above low water, enclosed a parade ground of roughly 1 acre. Along four of the walls extended two tiers of arched gunrooms.

Spiking the guns at Fort Moultrie, just prior to departure for Fort Sumter, December 26, 1860. From Frank Leslie's Illustrated Newspaper, January 5, 1861.

Officers' quarters lined the fifth side—the 316.7-foot gorge. This wall was to be armed only along the parapet. Three-story brick barracks for the enlisted garrison paralleled the gunrooms on each flank. At the center of the gorge was the sally port. It opened on the 25½-foot-wide stone esplanade that extended the length of that wall and on a 171-foot wharf.

Fort Sumter was unfinished when, late in December, gathering events prompted its occupation by artillery troops. Eight-foot-square openings yawned in place of gun embrasures on the second tier. Of the 135 guns planned for the gunrooms and the open terreplein above, only 15 had been mounted. Most of these were "32 pounders"; none was heavier. Various details of the interior finish of barracks, quarters, and gunrooms were incomplete. Congressional economies had had their effect, as much as difficulties of construction. As late as 1858 and 1859, work had been virtually at a standstill for lack of funds.

Major Anderson Moves Garrison from Moultrie to Sumter

On December 20, 1860, South Carolina seceded from the Union. On the night of the 26th, fearing attack by the excited populace, Maj. Robert Anderson removed the small garrison he commanded at Fort Moultrie to Fort Sumter out in the harbor. Ignorant of an apparent pledge to maintain the harbor *status quo*, given by President Buchanan some weeks before, Anderson moved in accordance with instructions received December 11, which read:

> ". . . you are to hold possession of the forts in this harbor, and if attacked you are to defend yourself to the last extremity. The smallness of your force will not permit you, perhaps, to occupy more than one of the three forts, but an attack on or attempt to take possession of any one of them will be regarded as an act of hostility, and you may then put your command into either of them which you may deem most proper to increase its power of resistance. You are also authorized to take similar steps whenever you have tangible evidence of a design to proceed to a hostile act."

Anderson thought he had "tangible evidence" of hostile intent, both towards Fort Moultrie—an old fort most vulnerable to land attack—and towards unoccupied Fort Sumter. He moved now "to prevent the effusion of blood" and because he was certain "that if attacked my men must have been sacrificed, and the command of the harbor lost." To Anderson, a Kentuckian married to a Georgia girl, preservation of peace was of paramount importance. At the same time, a veteran soldier of "unquestioned loyalty," he had a duty to perform.

Charleston was filled with excitement and rage. Crowds collected in the streets; military organizations paraded; and "loud and violent were the expressions of feeling against Major Anderson and his action."

There was almost as much consternation in Washington as in Charleston. Senators calling at the White House found President Buchanan greatly agitated. He stood by the mantelpiece, crushing a cigar in the palm of one hand, and stammered that the move was against his policy. The cabinet was called into session, and on December 27, Secretary of War Floyd wired Major Anderson:

> "Intelligence has reached here this morning that you have abandoned Fort Moultrie, . . . and gone to Fort Sumter. It is not believed, because there is no order for any such movement. Explain the meaning of this report."

South Carolina regarded Anderson's move not only as an "outrageous breach of faith," but as an act of aggression, and demanded, through commissioners, that the United States Government evacuate Charleston Harbor. President Buchanan, anxious to conciliate as well as maintain authority, wavered. Cabinet pressures were brought to bear. Meanwhile, on the 27th, South Carolina volunteers seized Castle Pinckney and Fort Moultrie. On the 28th, the President refused to accede to South Carolina's demand.

The North was exultant. Amid cheers for Major Anderson, salvos of artillery resounded in northern cities on New Year's Day, 1861. By

Maj. Robert Anderson. From Lossing, *A History of the Civil War.*

an imposing majority, the House of Representatives voted approval of Major Anderson's "bold and patriotic" act.

At Fort Sumter, Major Anderson had two companies of the First United States Artillery—about 85 officers and men in a fortification intended for as many as 650. He had only "about 4 months" supply of provisions for his command. The question of reenforcement and supply was to trouble all the remaining days of the Buchanan administration and to carry over to the succeeding administration. In it were the seeds of war.

The Star of the West

President Buchanan was persuaded to send off a relief expedition almost immediately. Initial plans called for the dispatch of the sloop of war *Brooklyn* for this purpose, but when word came which indicated that the South Carolinians had obstructed the harbor entrance by sinking several ships, it was decided to use an ordinary merchant ship. The *Brooklyn,* of heavy draft, could probably not now pass into the harbor. A merchant ship would certainly excite less suspicion and would avoid the appearance of a coercive movement. Accordingly, the *Star of the West*—a ship which regularly sailed southward from New York—was chartered. Two hundred men, small arms and ammunition, and several months' provisions were placed aboard. The men were to remain below deck on entering Charleston Harbor; the *Brooklyn* would follow, in case the *Star of the West* were fired upon and disabled.

But Charleston was forewarned. When the *Star of the West* appeared at the entrance of the harbor on January 9, 1861, Citadel cadets opened fire

The Star of the West. From *Battles and Leaders of the Civil War.*

with a gun mounted on Cummings Point; and the merchant ship, unarmed, steamed out of the harbor. Anderson had held his fire, thinking the firing unauthorized by the State authorities. Orders authorizing supporting fire on his part had failed to reach him in time. As if accidentally, civil war had been averted for the moment.

There was some Northern reaction to the incident, but further plans for Anderson's relief, once projected, were delayed. Anderson indicated no immediate need, and President Buchanan was anxious to end his term of office in peace. On January 10, the Secretary of War had ordered Major Anderson to act "strictly on the defensive." Anderson and Governor Pickens of South Carolina exchanged angry letters, and the Governor's demand for the fort's surrender (January 11) was resolved in the "mission" to Washington of the State's attorney general, I. G. Hayne. When that mission, tempered by the efforts of cooler-headed Southern Senators, met stubborn resistance on the part of President Buchanan, the situation was resolved in the formation of the Southern Confederacy, with the consequent assumption of the Fort Sumter problem by that government.

Preparations for War

Fort Sumter was now preparing for attack. Thirty-eight more guns were mounted in the first tier of casemates and along the parapet, including heavier "42 pounders" and Columbiads. Five Columbiads were mounted in the parade as mortars and three howitzers about the sally port in the gorge. By April 12, a total of 60 guns was ready. "Bombproof" shelters and "splinter-proof" traverses were constructed on the parade ground and along the parapet. Overhanging galleries were built out from the parapet at strategic points for dropping shells on an assaulting force. Special protection was given the gateway. Left unarmed, however, was the second tier of casemates; the 8-foot-square openings in the outer wall were bricked up. The small size of Major Anderson's garrison did not permit manning it.

Charleston, too, prepared. In addition to routine preparations at Castle Pinckney and Fort Moultrie, additional batteries were prepared on Sullivan's Island, at Cummings Point on Morris Island, and outside Fort Johnson. An "ironclad" Columbiad battery, constructed of inclined logs plated with iron, was mounted at Cummings Point. Meanwhile, Governor Pickens permitted Anderson to buy fresh meat and vegetables in town to supplement his garrison "issue" supply.

On February 4, 1861, delegates from six seceding States—South Carolina, Georgia, Florida, Alabama, Mississippi, and Louisiana—had met at Montgomery, Ala., to form the Confederate government. A constitution had been adopted and Jefferson Davis, of Mississippi, had been elected President and inaugurated on February 18. Texas came into the Confederacy on March 2. By this time all forts, arsenals, and navy yards in the seceding States had been seized by the Confederate government without resistance, except Fort Pickens on Pensacola Bay in Florida, two minor forts (Jefferson and Taylor) on and near the Florida coast, and Fort Sumter. Because of its association with the "hotbed of secession" and because of Major Anderson's dramatic move, Fort Sumter had assumed undeserved importance.

On March 3, Brig. Gen. P. G. T. Beauregard took command of the Confederate troops at Charleston. Like Major Anderson, Beauregard was a veteran of the Mexican War. He was a member of a Louisiana family of distinguished French lineage. Late captain in the United States Army, he had served briefly as superintendent of the United States Military Academy at West Point as recently as January. Once, years back, he had studied artillery there under Major Anderson; now, pupil confronted master.

Lincoln Orders a Relief Expedition to Fort Sumter

On March 4, Abraham Lincoln assumed office as President of the United States. In a firm, but generally conciliatory, inaugural address, he made it clear that national authority must be upheld against the threat of disunion. As to the Federal forts and property in the seceded States he said: "The power confided to me will be used to hold, occupy, and possess the property and places belonging to the Government. . . ." He did not say "repossess." Furthermore, there needed to be "no bloodshed or violence" as the result of this policy "unless it be forced upon the national authority." The President concluded:

Confederate preparations at Cummings Point, Morris Island. The inclined Ironclad Battery is at the left. From Frank Leslie's Illustrated Newspaper, March 30, 1861.

In the face of war preparations, wives and children leave Fort Sumter, February 3, 1861. From Frank Leslie's Illustrated Newspaper, February 23, 1861.

"In your hands, my dissatisfied fellow-countrymen, and not in mine, is the momentous issue of civil war. The Government will not assail you. You can have no conflict without being yourselves the aggressors. You have no oath registered in Heaven to destroy the Government, while I shall have the most solemn one to 'preserve, protect, and defend' it."

The Sumter situation was placed squarely before Lincoln on the day he assumed office. On the morning of Inaugural Day the outgoing Secretary of War received a dispatch from Major Anderson at Fort Sumter indicating that the remainder of the "issue" rations brought over from Fort Moultrie in December would last only a few more weeks. Meanwhile, in the face of local preparations, an estimated force of 20,000 men would now be needed to reenforce and supply Fort Sumter. It was clear that if Anderson's local "fresh food" supply were cut off, he would soon be in a desperate state. At the same time, it seemed almost equally clear that a relief expedition would be an impossibility. The entire Army of the United States numbered less than 16,000 men. "Evacuation seems almost inevitable," wrote General Scott; the majority of Lincoln's Cabinet agreed. But Lincoln investigated further. In the meantime, reassured

Brig. Gen. Pierre Gustave Toutant Beauregard. Courtesy National Archives.

by Secretary of State Seward as well as by others, the South came to believe Fort Sumter would be evacuated.

On April 4, President Lincoln sent word to Major Anderson that an attempt would be made to supply Fort Sumter with provisions "and, in case the effort is resisted . . . to reenforce you." Convinced from "on the spot" reports that such an expedition was feasible, and that there was no Union sentiment in South Carolina to which to appeal, Lincoln had decided upon the nearest thing to preserving the *status quo.* Merchant steamers under cover of ships of war would carry "subsistence and other supplies" to Anderson; the ships of war (with troop reenforcements) would be used only if a peaceable landing were opposed. Capt. G. V. Fox, long an advocate of a relief expedition, would command. Meanwhile, in accordance with pledge already given, the Governor of South Carolina would be carefully informed in advance.

The announcement of the expedition to supply Fort Sumter was the spark that set off the explosive forces which had been building up since 1850. The Confederate capital at Montgomery was informed. Anderson's "fresh" provision supply had already been cut off on the 7th; now, his mail was seized.

Work was pushed on the harbor fortifications. A new battery mounting two "24 pounders" and two "32 pounders" was unmasked on Sullivan's Island; another ironclad battery was put into position at its western tip. Originally designed to be "floating," this battery mounted two heavy "42 pounders" in addition to two "32 pounders." Near Mount Pleasant another (10-inch) mortar battery was installed. At Fort Moultrie, 11 guns now bore on Fort Sumter, including three 8-inch Columbiads. Additional guns were mounted to command the channels and to guard against landings by the fleet. Three thousand more troops were called, to be added to the 3,700 already on the post. The harbor seethed with activity.

"The gage is thrown down," said the Charleston *Mercury*, "and we accept the challenge. We will meet the invader, and God and Battle must decide the issue between the hirelings of Abolition hate and Northern tyranny, and the people of South Carolina defending their freedom and their homes."

Now, just in time, a small (12-pounder Blakely) rifled gun arrived from England as a gift of a Charlestonian, resident in London. It was mounted at Cummings Point, ominous forerunner of the powerful rifled guns that 2 years later would reduce Fort Sumter to ruin.

The Confederates Demand Fort Sumter's Evacuation

After cabinet debate in Montgomery, the Confederate Secretary of War ordered General Beauregard to demand the evacuation of the fort, and if that demand were refused, to "reduce it." On the afternoon of April 11, three of Beauregard's aides visited the fort under a flag of truce and presented the ultimatum. Major Anderson refused compliance, but at the

Artist's conception of the Confederate floating battery. The structure at the right was designed to be a hospital. From Frank Leslie's Illustrated Newspaper, March 30, 1861.

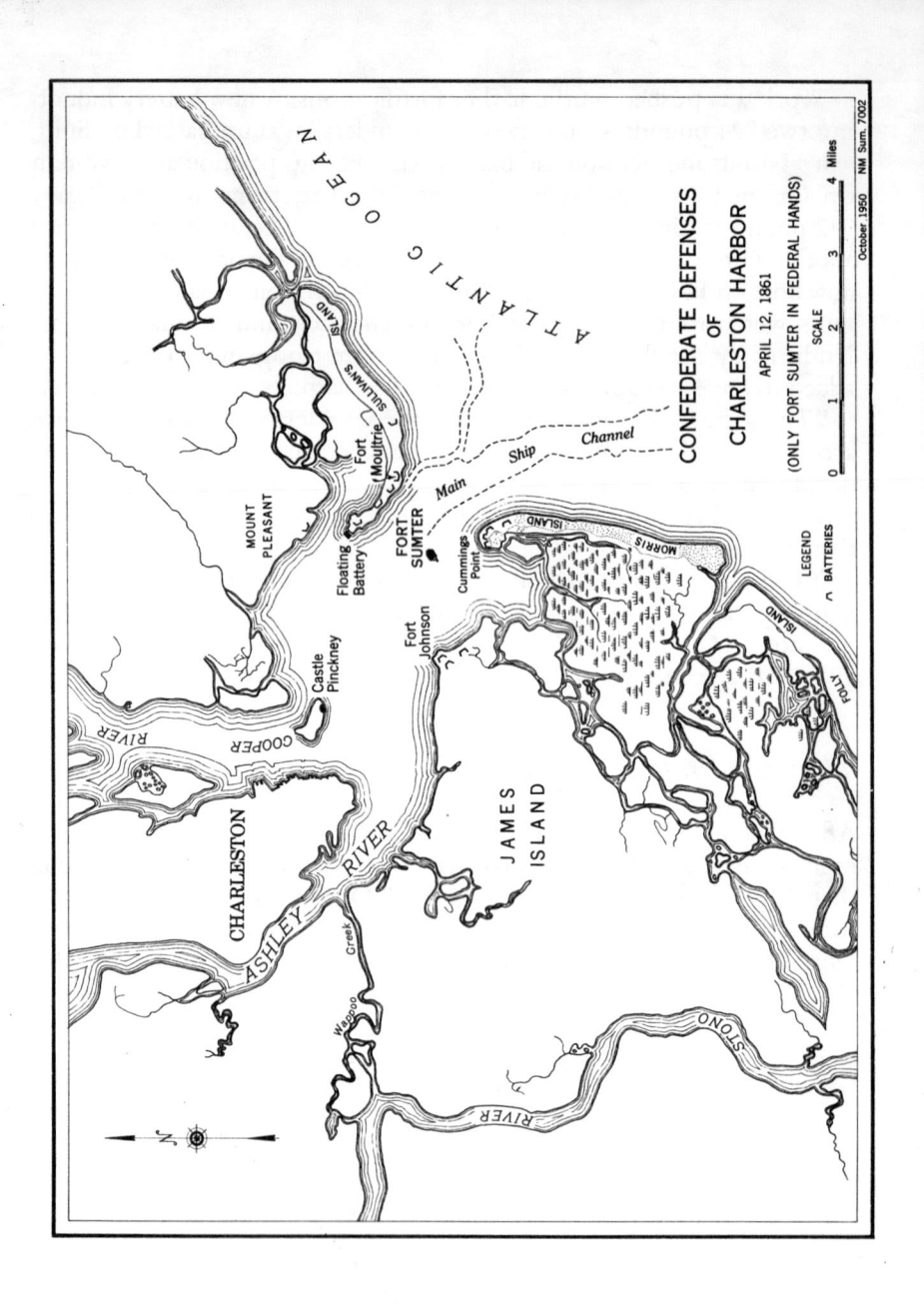

same time he said, "Gentlemen, if you do not batter the fort to pieces about us, we shall be starved out in a few days." Still reluctant to initiate conflict, the Montgomery government telegraphed:

"Do not desire needlessly to bombard Fort Sumter. If Major Anderson will state the time at which . . . he will evacuate, and agree that in the meantime he will not use his guns against us unless ours should be employed against Fort Sumter, you are authorized thus to avoid the effusion of blood. If this or its equivalent be refused, reduce the fort. . . ."

The atmosphere in Charleston was tense. In at least one household, dinner was the "merriest, maddest . . . yet. Men were more audaciously wise and witty. We had an unspoken foreboding it was to be our last pleasant meeting."

Shortly after midnight, four Confederate officers confronted Major Anderson again. About 3 hours later, in a carefully worded reply, the Union commander agreed to evacuate "by noon on the 15th" unless he should receive prior to that time "controlling instructions from my Government or additional supplies." But it was expected in Charleston that the Federal supply ships would arrive before the 15th. Major Anderson's reply was rejected by the Confederate officers, who proceeded at once to Fort Johnson to give the order to open fire.

The War Begins—April 12, 1861

"I count four by St. Michael's chimes, and I begin to hope. At half past four, the heavy booming of a cannon! I sprang out of bed and on my knees, prostrate, I prayed as I never prayed before."

At 4:30 a. m., a mortar at Fort Johnson fired a shell which arched across the sky and burst almost directly over Fort Sumter. This was the signal for opening the bombardment. Within a few minutes, a ring of guns and mortars about the harbor—43 in all—were firing at Sumter.

Artist's conception of the bombardment of Fort Sumter, April 12, 1861. Fort Johnson is in the foreground. From Harper's Weekly, April 27, 1861.

Major Anderson withheld fire until about 7 o'clock. Then Capt. Abner Doubleday, of latter-day baseball fame, fired a shot at the Ironclad Battery on Cummings Point. Ominously, the light shot "bounded off from the sloping roof . . . without producing any apparent effect." Not at any time during the battle did the guns of Fort Sumter do great damage to the Confederate defenses. Most of Fort Sumter's heaviest guns were on the parapet and in the parade, and, to reduce casualties in the small garrison, Major Anderson ordered these left unmanned. For a while, with the help of the 43 engineer workmen remaining at the fort, 9 or 10 of the casemate guns were manned. But by noon, the expenditure of ammunition was so much more rapid than the manufacture of new cartridge bags that the firing was restricted to 6 guns only. Meanwhile

"Showers of balls from 10-inch Columbiads and 42 pounders, and shells from [10] inch mortars poured into the fort in one incessant stream, causing great flakes of masonry to fall in all directions. When the immense mortar shells, after sailing high in the air, came down in a vertical direction, and buried themselves in the parade ground, their explosion shook the fort like an earthquake."

All Charleston watched. Business was entirely suspended. King Street was deserted. The Battery, the wharves and shipping, and "every steeple and cupalo in the city" were crowded with anxious spectators. And "never before had such crowds of ladies without attendants" visited the streets of Charleston. "The women were wild" on the housetops. In the darkness before dawn there were "Prayers from the women and imprecations from the men; and then a shell would light up the scene." As the

Preparing to fire the first shot from Fort Sumter, April 12, 1861. Contemporary artist's conception. Courtesy Charleston Library Society.

The bombardment of Fort Sumter, April 13, 1861.

day advanced, the city became rife with rumors: "Tonight, they say, the forces are to attempt to land. The *Harriet Lane* had her wheel house smashed and put back to sea. . . . We hear nothing, can listen to nothing. Boom boom goes the cannon all the time. The nervous strain is awful. . . ." Volunteers rushed to join their companies. There was "Stark Means marching under the piazza at the head of his regiment . . . ," his proud mother leaning over the balcony rail "looking with tearful eyes." Two members of the Palmetto Guards paid $50 for a boat to carry them to Morris Island.

The barracks at Fort Sumter caught fire three times that first day, but each time the fire was extinguished. One gun on the parapet was dismounted; another damaged. The wall about one embrasure was shattered to a depth of 20 inches. That was the Blakely rifle, in part, firing with "the accuracy of a duelling pistol." The quarters on the gorge were completely riddled. When night descended, dark and stormy, Fort Sumter's fire ceased entirely. With the six needles available, the work of making cartridge bags went forward; blankets, old clothing, extra hospital sheets,

Col. Louis T. Wigfall. From Mrs. D. Giraud Wright, *A Southern Girl in '61.* Courtesy Doubleday & Company.

and even paper, were used in the emergency. In the meantime, the supply fleet, off the bar since the onset of hostilities, did no more than maintain its position. It had been crippled upon departure when Seward's meddling had caused withdrawal of the powerful warship *Powhatan.* Now, bad weather prevented even a minimum supporting operation.

On the morning of the 13th, Sumter opened "early and spitefully," and, with the increased supply of cartridges, for a while kept up a brisk fire. About midmorning hot shot set fire to the officers' quarters. The Confederate fire then increased; soon the whole extent of the quarters was in flames; the powder magazines were in danger. The blaze spread to the barracks. By noon the fort was almost uninhabitable. The men crowded to the embrasures for air or lay on the ground with handkerchiefs over their mouths. For a time the fort continued to fire; valiant efforts had saved some of the powder before the onrush of the flames forced the closing of the magazines. Meanwhile, at every shot, the Confederate troops, "carried away by their natural generous impulses," mounted the different batteries and "cheered the garrison for its pluck and gallantry and hooted the fleet lying inactive just outside the bar."

About 1:30 in the afternoon the flag was shot down. Almost accidentally, this led to surrender. By authority of General Simons, commanding

Interior of Fort Sumter after the bombardment of April 1861. The Left Flank barrack is at the left; the Left Face is at the right. From G. S. Crawford, *The Genesis of the Civil War.*

Interior of the Gorge after the April 1861 bombardment. Parade entrance to sally port is at center.

on Morris Island, Col. Louis T. Wigfall, one of General Beauregard's aides detached for duty at that spot, set out by small boat to ascertain whether Major Anderson would capitulate. Till recently, Wigfall had been United States Senator from Texas. Before he arrived at the beleaguered fort, the United States flag was again flying, but Wigfall continued on. The firing continued from the batteries across the harbor. Once through an embrasure on the Left Flank, white handkerchief on the point of his sword, Colonel Wigfall offered the Federal commander any terms he desired, only "the precise nature of which" would have to be arranged with General Beauregard. Anderson accepted on the basis of Beauregard's original terms: evacuation with his command, taking arms and all private and company property, saluting the United States flag as it was lowered, and being conveyed, if desired, to a Northern port. The white flag went up again; the firing ceased. Wigfall departed confident that Anderson had surrendered unconditionally. He and his boatman were borne ashore "in triumph."

Meanwhile, officers had arrived at the fort direct from General Beauregard's headquarters in Charleston. From these men, dispatched to offer assistance to the Federal commander, Anderson learned that Wigfall's action was unauthorized; that, indeed, the colonel had not seen the Commanding General since the start of the battle. From another party

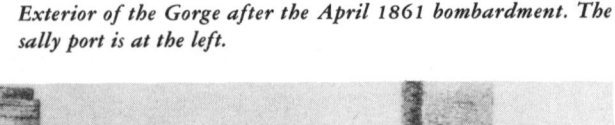

Exterior of the Gorge after the April 1861 bombardment. The sally port is at the left.

Rear Adm. Samuel F. Du Pont. From Johnson, *The Defense of Charleston Harbor.*

of officers he learned Beauregard's exact terms of surrender. They failed to include the privilege of saluting the flag, though in all other respects they were the same as those Anderson believed he had accepted from Wigfall. Impetuously, Anderson had first declared he would run up his flag again. Then, restrained by Beauregard's aides, he waited while his request for permission to salute the flag was conveyed to the Commanding General. In the course of the afternoon, General Beauregard courteously sent over a fire engine from the city. About 7:30 that evening, Beauregard's chief of staff returned with word that Major Anderson's request would be granted and the terms offered on the 11th would be faithfully adhered to. The engagement was officially at an end. During the 34-hour bombardment, more than 3,000 shells had been hurled at the fort.

On Sunday, April 14, Major Anderson and his garrison marched out of the fort with drums beating and colors flying and boarded ship to join the Federal fleet off the bar. On the 50th round of what was to have been a 100-gun salute to the United States flag, there occurred the only fatality

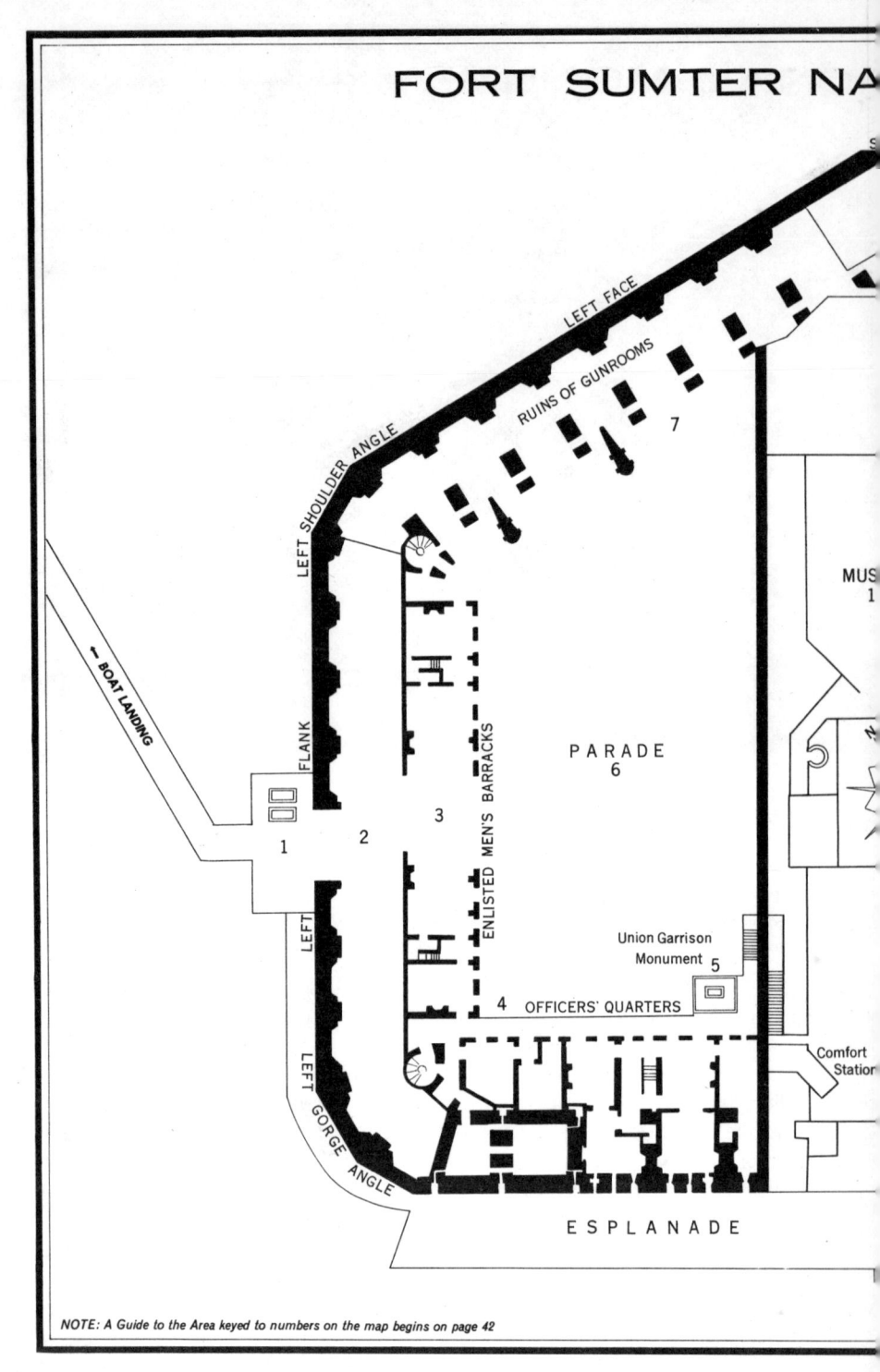

FORT SUMTER NA

LEFT FACE

RUINS OF GUNROOMS

7

LEFT SHOULDER ANGLE

BOAT LANDING

FLANK

1

2

3

ENLISTED MEN'S BARRACKS

PARADE
6

MUS
1

Union Garrison Monument 5

4 OFFICERS' QUARTERS

Comfort Station

LEFT

LEFT GORGE ANGLE

ESPLANADE

NOTE: A Guide to the Area keyed to numbers on the map begins on page 42

22

IONAL MONUMENT   SOUTH CAROLINA

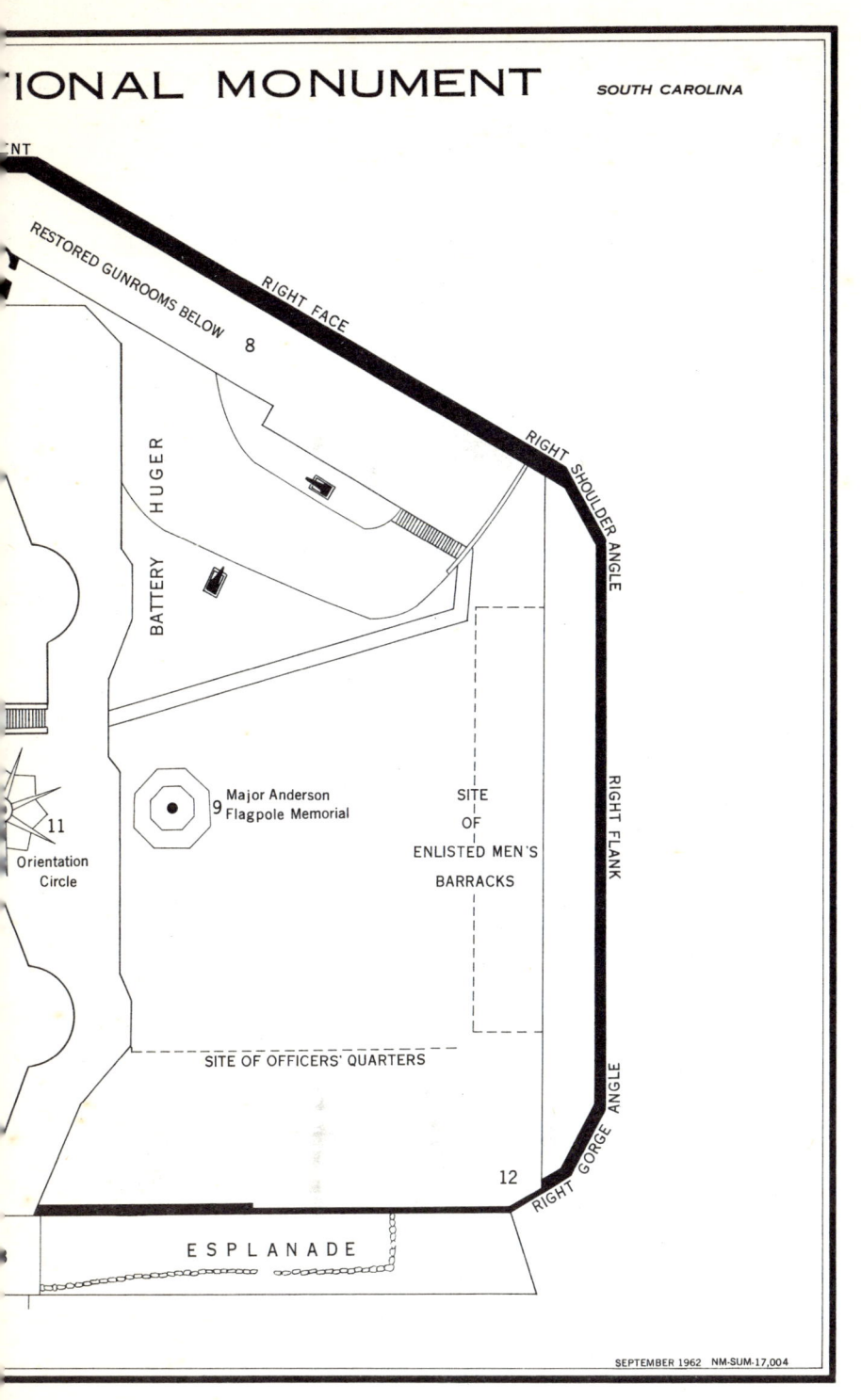

RESTORED GUNROOMS BELOW   8
RIGHT FACE
RIGHT SHOULDER ANGLE
RIGHT FLANK
RIGHT GORGE ANGLE

BATTERY HUGER

11
Orientation
Circle

9 Major Anderson
   Flagpole Memorial

SITE
OF
ENLISTED MEN'S
BARRACKS

SITE OF OFFICERS' QUARTERS

12

ESPLANADE

SEPTEMBER 1962   NM-SUM-17,004

23

of the engagement. The premature discharge of a gun and the explosion of a pile of cartridges resulted in the death of Pvt. Daniel Hough. Another man, mortally wounded, died several days later. The 50th round was the last. Now, as the steamer *Isabel* went down the channel, the soldiers of the Confederate batteries on Cummings Point lined the beach, silent, heads uncovered.

The following day, April 15, 1861, Abraham Lincoln issued a call for 75,000 militia. Civil war, so long dreaded, had begun. The States of Virginia, Arkansas, Tennessee, and North Carolina now joined the Confederacy.

Charleston and the Federal Blockade—1861-63

With Fort Sumter in Confederate hands, the port of Charleston became a most irritating loophole in the Federal naval blockade of the Atlantic coast—doubly irritating because at Charleston "rebellion first lighted the flame of civil war." As late as January 1863, it was reported that "vessels ply to and from Charleston and Nassau [Bahamas] with the certainty and promptness of a regular line." In 2 months of the spring following, 21 Confederate vessels cleared Charleston and 15 came in. Into Charleston came needed war supplies; out went cotton in payment.

Capture of Port Royal Harbor on November 7, 1861, by a Federal fleet under Capt. Samuel F. Du Pont, however, had made possible land and sea operations against Charleston. In June 1862, an attempt was made by Maj. Gen. D. H. Hunter to push through to Charleston by James Island on the south. This ended in Union disaster at Secessionville. Meanwhile, the *Monitor-Merrimac* action in Hampton Roads had indicated the feasibility of a naval "ironclad" expedition against Fort Sumter, the key to the harbor. Sumter, now largely rebuilt, had become a formidable work armed with some 95 guns and garrisoned with upwards of 500 men. In May 1862, the Navy Department had determined to capture Charleston "as soon as Richmond falls." To Du Pont, who was now rear admiral, there seemed to be a "morbid appetite in the land to have Charleston." The War Department, meanwhile, far from supplying additional troops to General Hunter's command in South Carolina, withdrew units to reenforce General McClellan in Virginia.

Federal Ironclads Attack Fort Sumter

On April 5, 1863, a fleet of 9 Federal ironclads, armed with 32 guns "of the heaviest calibres ever used in war," appeared off Charleston bar. Seven were of the single-turret "cheesebox on a raft" monitor type; one was a double-turreted affair; the flagship *New Ironsides* was an ironclad frigate. With the ebb tide, on the afternoon of the 7th, the "newfangled" ironclads steamed single file up the main ship channel east of Morris Island.

Contemporary artist's conception of Ironclad attack, April 7, 1863. The flagship New Ironsides *is at left center.* From Harper's Weekly, May 2, 1863.

The weather was clear and bright; the water "as stable as of a river." By 3 o'clock, the *Weehawken*, the leading monitor, had come within range, and Fort Moultrie opened fire. The *Passaic*, second in line, responded. Fort Sumter held fire, guns trained on a buoy at the turn of the channel. When the *Weehawken* came abreast of that point, all the guns atop Sumter's right flank let loose, followed by all the guns on Sullivan's Island, at Fort Moultrie, and at Cummings Point that could be brought to bear.

It was too much for the ironclads, slow and unwieldy, possessed of limited vision, and operating in a narrow and uncertain channel. In the course of the 2½-hour fight, only one came as close as 900 yards to Fort Sumter. To the 2,209 rounds hurled against them, the ironclads were able to return only 154, of which only 34 found the target. These breached and loosened the right flank parapet for a length of 25 feet and pocked the walls elsewhere with craters up to 2½ feet deep. But it was far from enough; Fort Sumter remained strong and secure. In the meantime, five of the ironclads were seriously disabled by the accurate fire, and one, the *Keokuk*, sank the following morning in the shallow water off Morris Island. In a daring exploit sometime later, Confederate troops recovered the guns of the *Keokuk* and mounted one at Fort Sumter.

Admiral Du Pont had "attempted to take the bull by the horns but had failed." The North, so confident of victory, was stunned at a time when the general military situation gave cause for gloom. The war in the East had been bloody and indecisive till now; the news from the West was bad.

Federal authorities looked to a combined operation to seize Morris Island and from there demolish Fort Sumter. With Fort Sumter reduced, the harbor could be entered.

The Morris Island Approach to Fort Sumter

Folly Island and Cole's Island, next south of Morris Island, had been occupied by Northern troops just prior to the naval attack. In June and July, the northern end of Folly Island was fortified. In a remarkable operation, 47 guns and mortars were secretly placed "within speaking distance of the enemy's pickets." Some 11,000 men were concentrated on the island. Brig. Gen. Quincy A. Gillmore, the "breacher" of Fort Pulaski, assumed command on June 12. Rear Adm. John A. Dahlgren superseded Admiral Du Pont on July 6.

During that time the Confederates mounted guns at the southern end of Morris Island and built up the earthworks at its upper end—Battery Gregg at Cummings Point and Battery Wagner some 1,400 yards to the south. The latter work, commanding the island at its narrowest point, was made into a formidable "sand fort" mounting about 15 guns.

Fort Sumter, 1,390 yards distant from Battery Gregg, prepared for siege, too. Brick and stone masonry "counterforts," already built at each extremity of the esplanade as protection for the magazines, were now strengthened, and much of the remaining gorge exterior was sandbagged,

Col. Alfred Rhett. From Johnson, *The Defense of Charleston Harbor.*

Bvt. Maj. Gen. Quincy A. Gillmore. From Johnson, *The Defense of Charleston Harbor.*

or otherwise protected. The casemates on the right flank ("sea front") were filled with sand, and the rooms on the gorge were filled with damp cotton bales laid in sand. The upper-tier magazines were abandoned and filled with sandbags to protect the magazines below. Protective revetments and defensive devices of various sorts were introduced at various points throughout the fort. During this period the garrison was host at frequent intervals to officers on leave, citizens of Charleston, and even many ladies, who came to see the scars of the April battle, to admire the drill, or to observe the preparations. At the end of June 1863, Fort Sumter was garrisoned with 5 companies (perhaps 500 men) of the First South Carolina Artillery, under the command of Col. Alfred Rhett. Its armament, meanwhile, had been reduced to 68 guns and mortars, many of the finest pieces having been removed to strengthen other fortifications about the harbor.

On the morning of July 10, 3,000 Union infantrymen, supported by the artillery on Folly Island and the guns of 4 monitors, descended on the southern end of Morris Island: Brig. Gen. Truman Seymour, a company commander at Fort Sumter 2 years before, commanded the assault. Within 4 hours, three-fourths of Morris Island was in his hands. Hopelessly outgunned and outmanned, the Confederate forces fell back to Battery Wagner. The guns of Fort Sumter helped to cover the retreat.

A "desperate" assault upon Wagner the following morning failed, though the parapet was briefly gained. General Gillmore established counterbatteries and tried again on the 18th. From noon until nightfall that day "without cessation or intermission," Federal guns poured a "storm of shot and shell upon Fort Wagner . . . perhaps unequalled in history"; then, some 6,000 troops assaulted—in the van, the 54th Massachusetts, "the first colored regiment of the North to go to war." In a short savage struggle, Seymour's force suffered 1,500 casualties. Though one angle of the fort was gained and held for a time, the attack was repulsed.

Thwarted in his plan to secure easy possession of Morris Island as a base for breaching operations against Fort Sumter, General Gillmore now determined to attempt that fort's reduction from the ground already in his possession. Batteries Wagner and Gregg would be taken by protracted siege operations. At Fort Sumter, removal of guns and ammunition continued apace. Anticipating that Sumter was "liable to be silenced sooner or later," and fearing attack at other points about the harbor, the Confederate authorities husbanded their resources. By mid-August, Fort Sumter's armament was reduced to a safe minimum of 38 guns and 2 mortars.

At distances of 2 to 2½ miles from Fort Sumter—distances extraordinary for such operations—Gillmore set up eight batteries of heavy rifled cannon. In the marsh west of Morris Island, where the mud was "like liquid," his engineers successfully emplaced a "200 pounder" to fire on Charleston; this was to be the notorious "Swamp Angel."

The first great breech in Fort Sumter's walls. Left Face interior, August 20, 1863. From an original photograph by G. S. Cook. Courtesy Mrs. T. R. Simmons, Charleston.

The First Great Bombardment of Fort Sumter

After some experimental firing starting August 12, the bombardment of Fort Sumter began in earnest on August 17. Nearly 1,000 shells were hurled at the fort that first day; nearly 5,000 more during the week following. Even at the end of the first day it was obvious that Fort Sumter was never intended to withstand "200 pound Yankee Parrotts." Then, 3 days later, a 13-ton monster throwing 250-pound shells was added, making 18 rifled cannon in action. Because of the range involved, the fort could not reply to the land batteries, and the monitors presented themselves only fleetingly.

On the 21st, with the "Swamp Angel" in position, Gillmore demanded the evacuation of Fort Sumter and Morris Island, threatening direct fire on the city of Charleston. Gillmore's ultimatum was unsigned, and General Beauregard was absent from his headquarters; but before confirmation could be secured, Gillmore had opened fire on the city. But little damage had been done when, on the 36th round, the "Swamp Angel" burst. Meanwhile, Beauregard had delivered an indignant reply. The bombardment of Fort Sumter continued.

By the 24th, General Gillmore was able to report the "practical demolition" of the fort. On that date, only one gun remained "serviceable in action." On the morning of the 23d, against Dahlgren's ironclads, Fort Sumter had fired what were to be its last shots in action. Its brick masonry walls were shattered and undermined; a breach 8 by 10 feet yawned in the upper casemates of the left face; at points, the sloped debris of the walls already provided a practicable route for assault.

Still, the Confederate garrison, supplemented by a force of 200 to 400 Negroes, labored night and day, strengthening and repairing. The debris, accumulating above the sand- and cotton-filled rooms, itself bolstered the crumbling walls. On August 26, General Beauregard ordered Fort Sumter held "to the last extremity."

The bombardment continued sporadically during the week following. On the night of September 1–2, the ironclads moved against the fort— the first major naval operation against Fort Sumter since the preceding April. Attempts earlier in the week had been thwarted by circumstance; now, conditions were right. For 5 hours, the frigate *New Ironsides* and five monitors bombarded the fort, now without a gun with which to reply to the "sneaking sea-devils." Two hundred and forty-five shot and shell were hurled against the ruin—twice as many as were thrown in the April attack. Then, tidal conditions, as much as a "rapid and sustained" fire from Fort Moultrie, forced the monitors' withdrawal.

Maj. Stephen Elliott. From Johnson, *The Defense of Charleston Harbor.*

Shell from the monitor Weehawken *exploding on the interior of Fort Sumter, September 8, 1863.* From an original photograph by G. S. Cook, Courtesy Charleston Chapter No. 4, United Daughters of the Confederacy.

Some desultory firing on the 2d brought to a close the first sustained bombardment of Fort Sumter. Over 7,300 rounds had been hurled against the fort since the opening of fire on August 17. With the fort, to all intents, reduced to a "shapeless and harmless mass of ruins," the Federal commanders now concentrated on Battery Wagner, to which General Gillmore's sappers had come within 100 yards.

On the morning of September 5, Federal cannoneers commenced a devastating barrage against that work. For 42 hours, night and day, in a spectacle "of surpassing sublimity and grandeur," 17 mortars and 9 rifled cannon, as well as the powerful guns of the ironclads, pounded the earthwork. Calcium lights "turned night into day." On the night of September 6–7, the Confederate garrisons at Wagner and Gregg evacuated; Morris Island, after 58 days, was at last in the hands of Union troops. Just three-quarters of a mile away stood Fort Sumter.

Sumter remained defiant. When Admiral Dahlgren demanded the fort's surrender, on the morning of the 7th, General Beauregard sent word that the admiral could have it when he could "take it and hold it." On September 4 the garrison had been relieved with fresh troops—320 strong. Maj. Stephen Elliott succeeded to the command.

Admiral Dahlgren "immediately designed to put into operation a plan to capture Fort Sumter." As a preliminary, the monitor *Weehawken* was ordered to pass in around Cummings Point "to cut off all communication by that direction." Later in the day, the *New Ironsides* and the remaining ironclads were to move up "to feel, and if possible, pass" the obstructions believed to be in the channel north of Sumter. But the *Weehawken* grounded, and the monitors caught such a severe fire from Fort Moultrie and the other Confederate batteries on Sullivan's Island, that Admiral Dahlgren "deemed it best to give [his] entire attention to the *Weehawken*" and withdraw. Whatever his original plan, Admiral Dahlgren now determined upon a small-boat assault. The task seemed simple; there was "nothing but a corporal's guard in the fort . . . all we have to do is go and take possession."

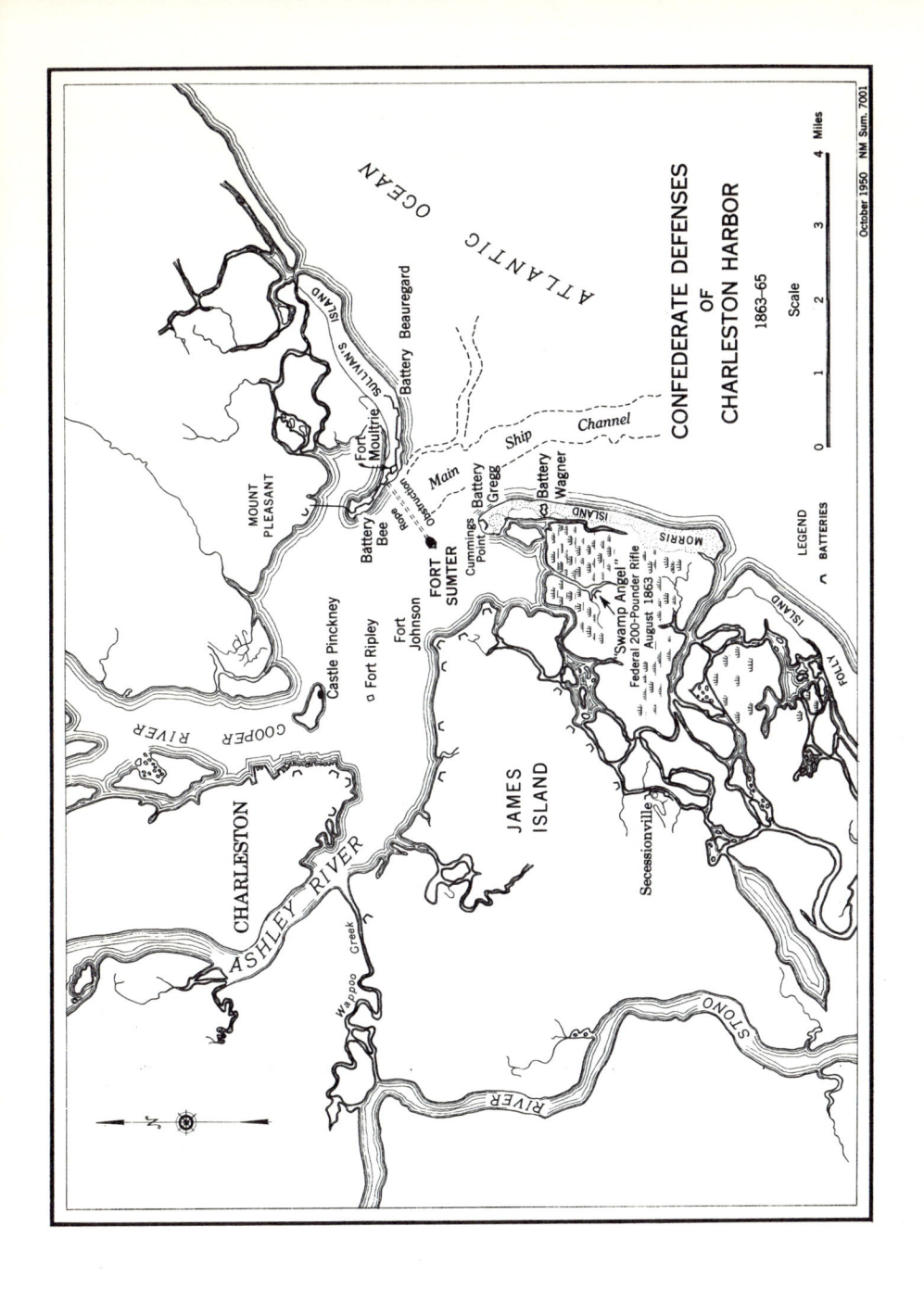

The Small-boat Assault

On the night of September 8–9, 400 sailors and marines made the attempt. A tug towed the small boats within 800 yards of the fort, then, too awkwardly, cast them loose. In the darkness and confusion, plans went awry. Without the benefit of a diversionary assault, two columns advanced simultaneously upon the right flank of the fort.

The Confederate garrison coolly held fire till the leading boats were in the act of landing, then let loose with a galling fire of musketry, hand grenades, "fire balls," grape and canister, brickbats, and masonry fragments. At a signal from the fort, the Confederate gunboat *Chicora* steamed out from the harbor and opened fire; Fort Moultrie "fired like a devil."

From the outer boats, the marines replied rapidly for a few minutes. Some of the sailors ashore fired a few times from their revolvers, but for the most part sought refuge in the embrasures or breaches of the wall. It was all over in 20 minutes. Most of the boats did not even touch shore. The Federal loss was 124 killed, wounded, and captured; 5 boats were taken. A similar expedition from Gillmore's command was detained by low tide in a creek west of Morris Island. Service rivalry had prevented active cooperation that might have meant victory.

For 19 days following the small-boat assault, Fort Sumter was free of attack; then, after a 6-day bombardment of "minor" proportions, for 23 days more. Damages sustained by the monitors in the Morris Island operation, as much as fear of channel obstructions (a menace afterwards

"The Flag of Sumter, October 20, 1863" painted by Conrad Wise Chapman, Confederate artist. Courtesy Confederate Museum, Richmond.

"Fort Sumter from Fort Moultrie, November 10, 1863" painted by Conrad Wise Chapman. Courtesy Confederate Museum, Richmond.

proved greatly exaggerated) and Fort Moultrie's evidently increased firepower, made Admiral Dahlgren reluctant to make another move at this time. General Gillmore, engaged now in rebuilding and rearming the captured Confederate batteries on Cummings Point, thought he had accomplished his part of the operation. In his opinion, Fort Sumter was effectively reduced; its seizure and occupation would be a costly and unnecessary operation. Further offensive operations by his force had never been contemplated; and the reenforcements needed for such operations were not to be had. Indeed, with the "turn of the tide" at Vicksburg and Gettysburg, Charleston had suddenly become much less important.

Meanwhile, Fort Sumter's garrison was not idle. It was at this time that the great "central bombproof," with quarters for 100 men, was built out from the gorge interior and, in the remaining casemates of the right face, a new 3-gun battery mounted.

The Second Great Bombardment

On October 26, "on the strength of certain reports . . . that the enemy have recently been at work remounting some guns," Gillmore resumed the bombardment; at least Fort Sumter could be "kept down" while the Navy prepared. For the next 12 days, the concentration of fire was comparable to the great bombardment of the preceding August. But now, firing from the new batteries on Cummings Point, with range shortened to less than a mile, the effect was far greater. For the first time, 16 heavy mortars were in use—2 of them 8½-ton pieces (13-inch bore) throwing 200-pound projectiles. Their sharp, plunging fire was added to that of

12 Parrott rifles—the types already used so effectively against the fort—and 1 powerful Columbiad. In addition, 2 monitors, with guns "equal to a dozen" Parrotts, crossed fire with Gillmore's artillery.

Sumter's "sea front" (right flank), upright and relatively unscathed till then, was breached now for nearly half its length. The ramparts and arches of its upper casemates were cut down and the interior barracks demolished. The accumulated debris made ascent easy inside and out. Through the breach, the Federal guns took the channel fronts "in reverse." For the first time, these were exposed to direct fire; soon they were "cut and jagged." Still, the gorge ruin remained much the same; to Admiral Dahlgren, that "heap of rubbish" looked "invincible."

Night and day, Gillmore's batteries maintained a "slow fire" against Fort Sumter throughout November and into December. On occasion the monitors assisted. Sumter could return merely "harmless musketry"; only telescopic rifle sights made even that much possible. But, the "rebels" seemed "snug in the ruins"; and if Sumter was without guns, Confederate batteries on James and Sullivan's Islands kept up an irritating counterfire.

On November 6, the Confederate engineer at Fort Sumter reported the bombproofs (quarters) unhurt. Although the height of the mass of the fort was "diminishing visibly on the sides away from the city," still, "when it gets down to the lower casemates [he wrote] it will have become so thick from accumulated debris as to resist further battering." Two weeks later, Major Johnson found the fort stronger than ever, and

Capt. John C. Mitchel. From Johnson, *The Defense of Charleston Harbor.*

Capt. Thomas A. Huguenin. From Johnson, *The Defense of Charleston Harbor.*

casualties were "either among those carelessly exposing themselves, outside the bombproof, or obliged to do so when at work." Indeed, casualties had been surprisingly low—only 2 men had been killed in the bombardment of August and only 22 more since the start of the second great bombardment; 118 had been wounded. Major Johnson did not "apprehend being run out by the big guns"; his chief anxiety was over "exposure to assault from barges at night."

In mid-November such an attack seemed to be forthcoming. During the early hours of the 18th, the defenders of the fort had "four distinct alarms" as small boats approached within hailing distance; "all hands out each time and expecting a fight." On the following night, a force estimated at 250 men approached within 300 yards of the fort, only to be driven off by the muskets of the aroused garrison.

But General Gillmore had merely ordered a "reconnaissance . . . of the nature of a simulated attack, with a view to compel the garrison to show its strength." Nor would he make another attempt. The next move remained up to the Navy.

Admiral Dahlgren continued to make no move. In any event, he could not advance until the repairs on the monitors were finished. As late as January 1864 these still were not complete. Meanwhile, in the face of reports of greatly strengthened harbor fortifications other than Fort Sumter, and increasingly concerned over the nature of the harbor obstructions, he was reluctant now to move forward without additional monitors. Defeat was always possible, and defeat for the Union's "only ironclad squadron" might have serious consequences, not only for the blockade and Gillmore's command on Morris Island, but for future operations elsewhere along the coast. In the meantime, "substantial" advantages had already been gained; the blockade at Charleston was tighter with Morris Island in Federal hands. To all this, the Navy Department agreed. Elsewhere, however, the war gathered momentum. In November, the North won decisively at Chattanooga.

The additional monitors, always promised, never seemed to arrive. On December 5, General Gillmore stopped the bombardment of Fort Sumter begun 41 days earlier. There seemed no great advantage in continuing, and it required considerable ammunition.

Stalemate—Spring of 1864

The general had made his last sustained effort against the fort. On only four other days in December did he fire any rounds at all. During the 4 months he remained in command the firing was intermittent, never more than "minor" in character. Meanwhile, forthcoming operations in Virginia required all the troops available. On May 1, 1864, General Gillmore departed for Fort Monroe with 18,000 picked men and quantities of valuable matériel.

General Grant's operations required the services of the additional monitors awaited by Admiral Dahlgren. With the monitor force reduced to six by the foundering of the *Weehawken* in December, further offensive operations against Charleston seemed completely out of the question. In June, the ironclad frigate *New Ironsides* was withdrawn to the north.

Fort Sumter Strengthened

In the preceding December, Fort Sumter had been an "almost chaotic ruin." At night, below the "rugged outline of the ramparts," wrote one of the garrison, all was—

"dark with piles of disordered material; a chance shower of sparks blows out from smouldering fire and lights up some great rough blocks of brick work and the pools of stagnant water into which they have been violently thrown some days before. Or lanterns move about in unseen hands, some to light a way for long trains of men toiling with heavy timbers and bags of sand over the roughest footing and up steep and uncertain, tumbling slopes; some to direct the heaping of material over old damaged hiding places repaired for the twentieth time since the firing began, or to build up newer and more lasting shelters for the garrison. . . ."

With the fort practically left alone during the months immediately following, the garrison gradually restored order from chaos. The parade ground, excavated well below high-water level to provide sand-filling, was cleared, drained, and partially rebuilt. Trim ranks of gabions (wicker baskets filled with sand) bolstered the sloping debris of the walls on the interior. The three-gun battery in the lower right face was lined with logs and planks, 10 feet deep, and revetted more thoroughly in the rear. In casemates of the left flank another three-gun battery was created. Through the disordered debris of the left and right faces, the garrison tunneled a 275-foot timbered gallery connecting the two batteries and fort headquarters in the left flank. In from the rubble of the "sea front," the garrison built a loopholed timber blockhouse to cover the parade ground in the event of further assault. In May, Capt. John C. Mitchel, son of the Irish patriot, relieved Lt. Col. Stephen Elliott in command.

The Third Great Bombardment

The onset of summer, 1864, brought one more attempt to take Fort Sumter; likewise another officer of the original Fort Sumter garrison came into the operation. Maj. Gen. J. G. Foster, engineer of the fort in April 1861, succeeding to Gillmore's command on May 26, was convinced that "with proper arrangements" the fort could easily be taken "at any time." The "proper arrangements" included special light-draft steamers and 1,000-man "assaulting arks" equipped with elevated towers for sharpshooters and 51-foot scaling ladders. Though initial War Department reaction was cool, Foster went ahead with a preliminary

"Fort Sumter: Interior Sunrise, December 9, 1864" painted by Conrad Wise Chapman. Courtesy Confederate Museum, Richmond.

operation to complete the demolition of the fort. "Yankee ingenuity" might succeed where routine operations had failed or been judged too costly.

On July 7, 1864, Foster's batteries opened a sustained bombardment against the ruin of Fort Sumter. During the remainder of that month, an average of 350 rounds daily was hurled at the beleagured fort. In some respects, this was the heaviest bombardment Fort Sumter had yet received. Although the gorge ruin was wasted away at one point to within 20 feet of the water, and the shattered "sea front" was still further reduced, the right face remained erect, its three-gun battery intact, likewise most of the left flank. To Admiral Dahlgren, as late as July 21, the work seemed "nearly impregnable." Debris added to debris, feverish work day and night, and thousands of bags of sand brought from the city by night actually made the fort stronger than ever. If a casemate were breached, it was speedily filled; if the slopes of the ruin invited assault, a bristling array of wooden pikes and barbed-wire entanglements were provided; and there were always the muskets of the 300-man garrison.

The fire slackened in August; Foster's supply of ammunition was dwindling. A scheme for "shaking down" the fort walls by floating down large "powder rafts" failed miserably. Mid-August brought final War Department refusal to supply light-draft steamers; the end of August, sharp disapproval for Foster's "assaulting arks." Meanwhile, Admiral Dahlgren had been unwilling to cooperate in an alternate plan of assault.

With his requisitions for more ammunition unfilled, General Foster was now called upon to ship north most of his remaining ammunition and four more regiments of troops to be used in Grant's operations against Richmond. Foster was ordered to remain strictly on the defensive.

On September 4, the bombardment begun on July 7 came to an end. In the 61 days, another 14,666 rounds had been hurled against the fort. Sixteen of the garrison had been killed, 65 wounded. On July 20, Captain Mitchel fell mortally wounded. Capt. Thomas A. Huguenin succeeded him that night.

Sherman's March Forces Sumter's Evacuation

The last great bombardment of Fort Sumter had taken place. The firing was no more than desultory after September 1864; less than a hundred rounds were hurled at the fort in the months of December and January; none at all in February. During the autumn months it was all Foster's batteries could do to make a "decent defense" of Morris Island, let alone carry on any offensive operations. Wrote one of the commanders in mid-September:

"The shelling from the enemy's mortars was severe . . . and having but little mortar powder, we were unable to reply effectually. . . . I regret that our ordnance supplies are so scanty. . . . No powder for the mortars; no suitable fuses for the fire on Charleston; no shells for the 30-pounder Parrotts, a most useful gun for silencing the enemy's fire; no material for making cartridge bags, or grease for lubricating the projectiles. . . . More ammunition for the 300-pounder, the most useful guns in these works, is also very much needed. . . ."

And Sumter itself was more than irritating:

"Within the last 2 days the work . . . has been greatly interfered with by a corps of sharpshooters . . . stationed on Fort Sumter. The bullets came in very thick when I was at the front this morning. . . ."

In February 1865, the long stalemate came to an end. In that month, General Sherman commenced his march north from Savannah through the interior of South Carolina, slicing between the remnants of Hood's army on the west and the small Confederate force remaining along the coast. On the 17th, with Sherman in Columbia, Fort Sumter and the other Confederate fortifications in Charleston harbor were quietly evacuated. At 9 o'clock on the morning of the 18th, the United States flag was once more raised over Fort Sumter. The fortunes of war had accomplished what 3,500 tons of metal, a fleet of ironclads, and thousands of men had failed to do.

Major Anderson Returns

On April 14, 1865, Robert Anderson, now a retired brigadier general, returned to Fort Sumter to raise again the flag he had pulled down 4 years before. The guns of the harbor thundered in salute. In an address before the throng of spectators brought down from New York, Henry Ward Beecher said:

Raising the original flag at Fort Sumter, April 14, 1865. Contemporary artist's sketch from French and Cary, The Trip of the Steamer Oceanus to Fort Sumter.

"We raise our fathers' banner, that it may bring back better blessings than those of old, that it may cast out the devil of discord; that it may restore lawful government and a prosperity purer and more enduring than that which it protected before; that it may win parted friends from their alienation; that it may inspire hope and inaugurate universal liberty; . . . that it may heal all jealousies, unite all policies, inspire a new national life, compact our strength, purify our principles, ennoble our national ambitions, and make this people great and strong . . . for the peace of the world. . . ."

That night, with tragic coincidence, an assassin's bullet felled Abraham Lincoln in Washington.

Fort Sumter After 1865

In the 1870's the rubble and ruin of war were cleared from the interior of Fort Sumter, and the work of reconstruction began. The outer walls of the gorge and right flank, largely destroyed by the bombardments, were partially rebuilt. The other walls of the fort, left jagged and torn

Horizontal section, Fort Sumter, February 1865. The Gorge is at the base of the plan. Courtesy National Archives.

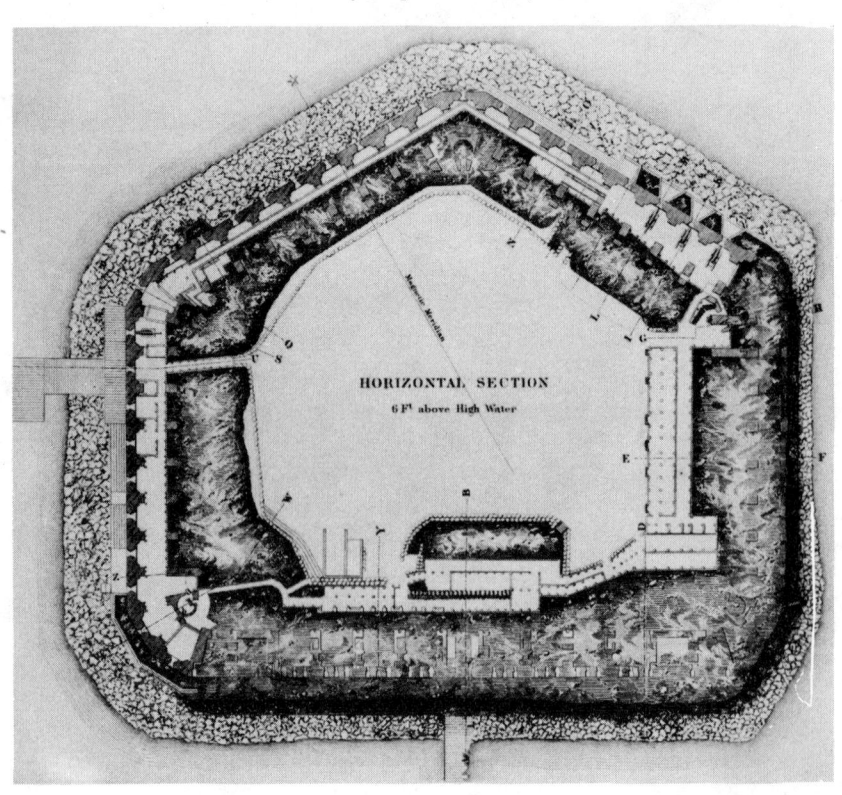

Interior of the Gorge as seen from atop the Left Flank, February 1865. The central bombproof is at the left.

30 to 40 feet above water, were leveled to approximately half their original height. Through the left flank a new sally port was constructed. Within the reconstructed walls of the fort, the earth and concrete works for a 10-gun battery *en barbette* (guns fired from an open parapet) began to take shape.

Operations were well advanced, when, in June 1876, shortage of funds forced complete suspension of activity. Only three permanent barbette platforms had been constructed by that time. Of necessity, seven temporary (wooden) platforms remained; on these, four "200 pounder" Parrott rifles and two 15-inch Rodman smoothbores had been mounted. In a modification of the original plan, 11 lower-tier gunrooms of the original fort along the right face and about the salient had been recovered and armed with "100 pounder" Parrotts. In a gradually deteriorating state, these 17 guns constituted Fort Sumter's armament for the next 23 years.

Exterior, Fort Sumter, February 1865. The Gorge is at the right; the Left Flank is at the left.

From 1876 to 1898, Fort Sumter stood largely neglected, important mainly as a lighthouse station. Ungarrisoned, most of that time it was in the charge of a "fortkeeper" or an ordnance sergeant. Without proper funds for maintenance, Fort Sumter, even then visited by thousands each year, fell into a state of dilapidation. By 1887 the wooden platforms of the barbette guns had rotted away so that "not one gun could be safely fired"; the neat earth slopes had eroded into "irregular mounds"; and quantities of sand had drifted into the parade ground. The casemate guns rusted so that they could not be traversed; salt water dashed freely through the open embrasures, the shutters of which were no longer in working order.

The Spanish-American War, 1898, prompted the construction in 1899 of a battery of two long-range rifled cannon at Fort Sumter. The massive concrete emplacement for this battery (named for Isaac Huger, South Carolinian, general in the American Revolution) dominates the central portion of Fort Sumter today. The guns, long since outmoded, were removed about 1941. During World War II, Fort Sumter was armed with 90-mm. antiaircraft guns manned by a garrison of Coast Artillery.

Guide to the Area

The following guide should be used with the map on pages 22 and 23. Numbers on the map correspond to the numbers in the text below.

One of the 12-inch guns of Battery Huger, as mounted in 1901.

1. LEFT-FLANK EXTERIOR. Entrance to Fort Sumter is by way of a modern sally port built through the center of the fort's left flank. This sally port, erected after the Civil War, replaced a gun embrasure. The two 13-inch mortars mounted outside this entry serve as the visitor's introduction to the ordnance now located at Fort Sumter. In 1863–65 Federal troops on Morris Island used this type of mortar against the fort. A marker on the left flank near the sally port honors the Confederate defenders of Fort Sumter.

2. LEFT-FLANK CASEMATES. The casemates (gunrooms) of the lower tier on the left flank were surmounted by a second tier identical in apperance. Above the second-tier casemates, guns were mounted *en barbette* on an open terreplein. This arrangement was also used on the fort's right flank and on its right and left faces. Each casemate contained one gun, which could be moved on a track for crossfiring through the embrasure. Fort Sumter was designed for an armament of 135 guns and a garrison of 650 men. There are now two guns mounted on the casemate carriages in the left flank. The one on the left of the sally port is a rifled and banded "42-pounder"; the one on the right is a 42-pound smoothbore. Shielded (by the mass of the gorge) from Federal guns on Morris Island, 1863–65, the left flank casemates were used as a Confederate headquarters and hospital. The lower half of the outer wall retained its full height until the end of the siege, but was leveled to approximately half its original height during the 1870's.

3. ENLISTED MEN'S BARRACKS. Inside and parallel to the left flank are the ruins of an enlisted men's barracks. This building, three stories high, rose slightly above the fort walls. The first floor contained the kitchen and mess facilities, with sleeping quarters on the two upper floors. Another barracks for enlisted men, identical to this one, was located on the right flank.

4. OFFICERS' QUARTERS. Along the gorge (or back wall) was another 3-story brick building, the officers' quarters. In addition to furnishing lodging to the officers of Fort Sumter, this building also housed the administrative offices, storerooms, powder magazines, and jail. Most of the wooden parts of the building burned during the initial Confederate bombardment. While the fort was in Confederate hands, many of the rooms were filled with sand and bales of cotton to strengthen the gorge.

5. GARRISON MONUMENT. The U.S. Government erected this monument in 1932 ". . . in memory of the garrison defending Fort Sumter during the bombardment April 12–14, 1861." The roster of the original garrison is listed on the tablet.

6. PARADE. In 1899, when Battery Huger was built in the center of the ruins of Fort Sumter, the remainder of the fort was filled with sand to strengthen it against guns of that period. In 1959 the National Park Service completed excavations that uncovered the entire left side of Fort Sumter down to the level of the original parade. Most of the fill on the right side is still in place.

7. LEFT FACE. Union guns destroyed the arched brick casemates of the left face during the Civil War. When Union gunners, firing on the gorge of Fort Sumter from Morris Island, aimed too high, their projectiles crossed the parade and struck the interior of the left face. Holes caused by these reverse shots, and even shells themselves, are still seen in the ruins of the left-face casemates. Just inside these casemates are two 15-inch smoothbore Rodman guns. They were part of Fort Sumter's post-Civil War armament.

8. RIGHT FACE. Guns mounted on the lower tier of this face dueled with Fort Moultrie in the initial attack, April 12–14, 1861. Since the angle of the face allowed it to escape broadsides from Federal batteries on Morris Island, its outer wall still stood almost at full height in February 1865. After Fort Sumter was silenced in August 1863, the Confederate garrison mounted three guns in the first-tier casemates just above the right shoulder angle. This was the "Palmetto Battery," called thus because of the protective log cover raised on the exterior. For several months this battery was the sole armament of the fort. All the lower-tier casemates were reclaimed in the 1870's and armed with "100-pounder" Parrott rifled cannon. These guns, rusted and worn, were buried with the casemates just before Battery Huger was constructed. To open these casemates, parade-ground excavations were extended into this part of the fort. Eleven 100-pound Parrott guns were uncovered and are now displayed in this face.

9. THE FLAGPOLE MONUMENT. The Fort Sumter flagpole is a monument honoring Major Anderson and his garrison. It was erected by Eba Anderson Lawton, daughter of Major Anderson, and accepted by Congress on May 11, 1928.

10. MUSEUM. Exhibits in the Fort Sumter Museum graphically relate the entire history of the fort. Informational literature and post cards can be obtained at the information desk. The gunroom for the 12-inch disappearing gun of Battery Huger was adapted to house the exhibits for this museum, which was dedicated April 12, 1961.

11. ORIENTATION CIRCLE. This point atop Battery Huger is almost in the center of old Fort Sumter. On either side are the 12-inch

100-pound Parrott guns uncovered in 1959 excavations.

gun emplacements of Battery Huger; the one toward the salient was converted into the museum. The area stretching out from this point to the right flank wall is earth fill, the height of which averages 20 feet above the original parade ground. In the center of the orientation circle is a model of Fort Sumter, oriented exactly with the fort.

12. RIGHT-GORGE ANGLE. From a gun in the first tier casemates, Capt. Abner Doubleday fired the first shot from Fort Sumter on April 12, 1861. Also in this section of the fort occurred the deepest penetration of Confederate shot and shell in the initial attack. In part, this was the work of the Confederates' rifled gun, the first one fired in action in America.

13. ESPLANADE. A 25½-foot-wide promenade and landing space once lined the full length of the gorge exterior at its base. Out from the center of the esplanade ran the original stone wharf, 171 feet long. Through the gorge, at the head of the wharf, was the original sally port to the fort.

Aerial view of Fort Sumter in January 1961.

Administration

Fort Sumter National Monument was established by Congress in 1948 and enlarged in 1961 with the acquisition of Fort Moultrie on Sullivans Island. The monument is administered by the National Park Service, U.S. Department of the Interior. Communications concerning the monument should be addressed to the Superintendent, Fort Sumter National Monument, U.S. Custom House, Charleston, S.C.

Related Areas

Other units of the National Park System pertaining to the Civil War are: Antietam National Battlefield Site, Md.; Appomattox Court House National Historical Park, Va.; Brices Cross Roads National Battlefield Site, Miss.; Chickamauga and Chattanooga National Military Park, Ga. and Tenn.; Fort Donelson National Military Park, Tenn.; Fredericksburg and Spotsylvania National Military Park, Va.; General Grant National Memorial, N.Y.; Gettysburg National Military Park, Pa.; Harpers Ferry National Monument, W. Va.; Kennesaw Mountain National Battlefield Park, Ga.; Manassas National Battlefield Park, Va.; Pea Ridge National Military Park, Ark.; Petersburg National Military Park, Va.; Richmond National Battlefield Park, Va.; Shiloh National Military Park, Tenn.; Stones River National Battlefield, Tenn.; and Vicksburg National Military Park, Miss.

Suggested Readings

CATTON, BRUCE, *The Coming Fury.* Doubleday & Co., Garden City, 1961.

CHESNUT, MARY B., *A Diary From Dixie.* Houghton Mifflin Co., Boston, 1949.

JOHNSON, ROBERT U., & CLARENCE C. BUEL, editors, *Battles and Leaders of the Civil War.* Reprint edition by Thomas Yoseloff, Inc., New York, 1956. Vols. I and IV.

STAMPP, KENNETH M., *And The War Came.* Louisiana State University Press, Baton Rouge, 1950.

SWANBERG, W. A., *First Blood.* Charles Scribner's Sons, New York, 1957.

UNITED STATES GOVERNMENT, *War of the Rebellion, A Compilation of the Official Records of the Union and Confederate Armies.* U.S. Government Printing Office, Washington, D.C., 1880. Series I, vols. I, XIV, XXVIII, and XXXV.